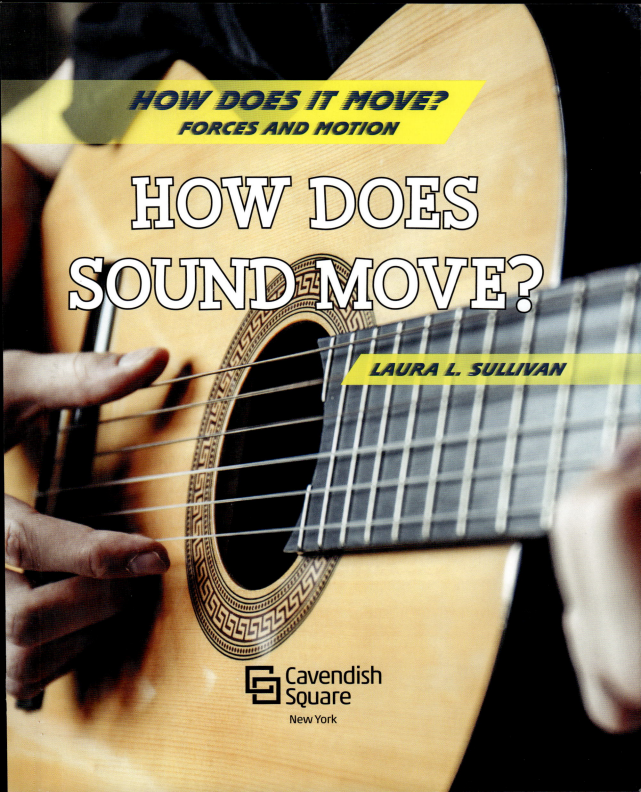

HOW DOES IT MOVE?
FORCES AND MOTION

HOW DOES SOUND MOVE?

LAURA L. SULLIVAN

Cavendish Square
New York

Published in 2019 by Cavendish Square Publishing, LLC
243 5th Avenue, Suite 136, New York, NY 10016

Copyright © 2019 by Cavendish Square Publishing, LLC

First Edition

No part of this publication may be reproduced, stored in a retrieval system, or transmitted in any form or by any means–electronic, mechanical, photocopying, recording, or otherwise–without the prior permission of the copyright owner. Request for permission should be addressed to Permissions, Cavendish Square Publishing, 243 5th Avenue, Suite 136, New York, NY 10016. Tel (877) 980-4450; fax (877) 980-4454.

Website: cavendishsq.com

This publication represents the opinions and views of the author based on his or her personal experience, knowledge, and research. The information in this book serves as a general guide only. The author and publisher have used their best efforts in preparing this book and disclaim liability rising directly or indirectly from the use and application of this book.

All websites were available and accurate when this book was sent to press.

Library of Congress Cataloging-in-Publication Data

Names: Sullivan, Laura L., 1974- author.
Title: How does sound move? / Laura L. Sullivan.
Description: First edition. | New York : Cavendish Square Publishing, [2019] | Series: How does it move? Forces and motion | Includes bibliographical references and index. | Audience: 2-5.
Identifiers: LCCN 2017054202 (print) | LCCN 2017059700 (ebook) | ISBN 9781502637864 (ebook) | ISBN 9781502637833 | ISBN 9781502637840 (pbk.)| ISBN 9781502637857 (6 pack) | ISBN 9781502637833 (library bound) | ISBN 9781502637857(6 pack)
Subjects: LCSH: Sound–Juvenile literature.
Classification: LCC QC225.5 (ebook) | LCC QC225.5 .S85 2019 (print) | DDC 534–dc23
LC record available at https://lccn.loc.gov/2017054202

Editorial Director: David McNamara
Editor: Meghan Lamb
Copy Editor: Michele Suchomel-Casey
Associate Art Director: Amy Greenan
Designer: Megan Mette
Production Coordinator: Karol Szymczuk
Photo Research: J8 Media

The photographs in this book are used by permission and through the courtesy of: Cover Dziewul/Shutterstock.com; p. 4 Valery Sidelnykov/Shutterstock.com; p. 6 Artpartner-images/Photographer's Choice/Getty Images; p. 7 Snapgalleria/Shutterstock.com; p. 8 Yann Hubert/Shutterstock.com; p. 9 Victor Habbick Visions/Science Photo Library/Getty Images; p. 10 ©iStockphoto/Wavebreak Media; p. 12 Stockshoppe/Shutterstock.com; p. 13 ©iStockphoto/Ysal; p. 14 Designua/Shutterstock.com; p. 15 Sunny/The Image Bank/Getty Images; p. 18 ©iStockphoto/Rypson; p. 19 (left) Alexandr III/Shutterstock.com; p. 19 (right) FreeSoulProduction/Shutterstock.com; p. 20 Naeblys/Shutterstock.com; p. 22 Dorling Kindersley/Getty Images; p. 23 Design Pics Inc/Alamy Stock Photo; p. 25 (top) Danita Delimont/Gallo Images/Getty Images; p. 25 (bottom) ©iStockphoto/Mladn61; p. 26 Evkaz/Shutterstock.com; p. 27 Diego Schtutman/Shutterstock.com.

Printed in the United States of America

CONTENTS

1 Surrounded by Sound 5

2 The Science of Sound 11

3 Sound Discoveries 21

   How Does It Move Quiz 28

   Glossary 29

   Find Out More 30

   Index 31

   About the Author 32

There are sounds all around!

CHAPTER 1

SURROUNDED BY SOUND

Close your eyes and listen to the sounds around you. You might hear other people talking. You might hear a show on television. You might hear birdsong outside. If it is very quiet, you might hear only the sound of your breathing. All of these sounds are very different, but they travel the same way.

All sounds are **vibrations**. A vibration is an up-and-down or back-and-forth movement. If you

Sound travels in a wave. Our ears are shaped to catch these waves.

drew a vibration, it would look like a long line of waves rising and falling. Traveling sound energy is called a sound wave.

Most animals can hear sounds. In humans, sounds travel first to the outer ear. Ears are shaped to catch sound waves.

HOW DO WE HEAR SOUND?

When a sound moves through your ear, it starts at a small tunnel called the **ear canal**. The sound moves through the ear canal until it hits the **eardrum**. The eardrum is a thin piece of skin stretched tight like a drum. It vibrates when sound hits it. Those vibrations are passed on to three ear bones. As sound waves bounce off the ear bones, the vibrations get bigger and bigger.

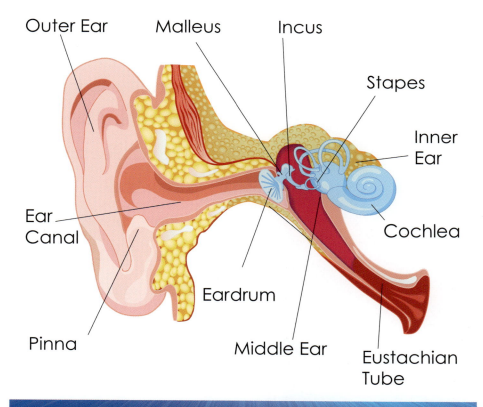

When vibrations hit the ear, the brain turns them into sounds we can understand.

FAST FACT

*Bats and whales use sounds to find their way in the dark. Bat squeaks and clicks bounce off of insects. When the sound bounces back, the bat can tell where the insect is. The bounce-back of a sound is called an **echo**. When animals use echoes to find their way, they are using echolocation.*

Sounds, such as whale songs, travel very well through water.

From there, the sound moves into the fluid-filled **cochlea**. The cochlea sends signals to your brain.

These signals travel through nerves. If you hear a voice, your brain can figure out who is talking and what they are saying.

Bats can "see" in the dark using sound echoes. This navigation process is called echolocation.

FAST FACT

An opera singer can shatter a glass with her voice. If she holds exactly the right note, she can make the glass vibrate until it breaks.

SURROUNDED BY SOUND

Sound science is important in the classroom—you need to hear your teacher!

CHAPTER 2

THE SCIENCE OF SOUND

Sounds are an important part of daily life. We use sound to express ideas when we speak. We use sound to create music. So much of our learning relies on sound. Hearing is one of our most important senses.

The movement of sound is part of our art. Music is all about making pleasing or interesting vibrations.

These vibrations can be made by instruments or the voice.

Sounds begin as movement. You strum a guitar chord. You beat a drum. When you sing or speak, the vocal cords in your throat move to create sound.

Sounds play an important role in scientific exploration and medicine. **Sonar** (sound navigation and ranging) is a technology that uses sound echoes to

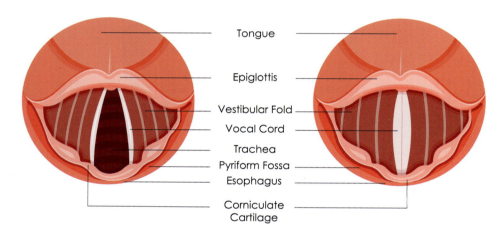

Tongue
Epiglottis
Vestibular Fold
Vocal Cord
Trachea
Pyriform Fossa
Esophagus
Corniculate Cartilage

VOCAL CORD

Speaking and singing start with vibrations of the vocal cords.

navigate or find objects. Scientific vessels explore the ocean floor or discover artifacts using sound. Doctors use a technology called the **ultrasound**. An ultrasound sends sound waves inside the human body. This allows doctors to look at a baby inside its mother or to find certain diseases such as cancer.

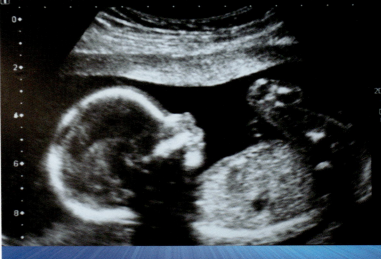
Sound can be used to view a baby inside its mother.

SOUND AND MATTER

Sound vibrations travel through **matter**. Matter is anything that takes up space. The matter through which sound travels is called a **medium**. The medium can be gas, liquid, or solid.

Sounds move more easily through some mediums than others. In gases, such as the air we breathe, the molecules are farther apart. Molecules are tiny parts that make up all matter.

It is harder for the sound wave to move from one molecule to the next. However, in liquids the molecules

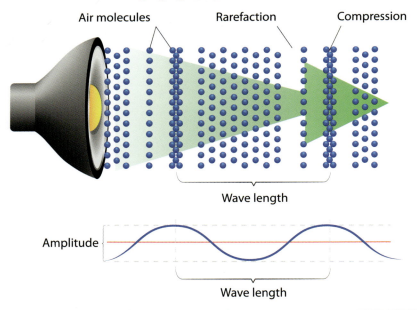

Amplitude is a measure of a sound's loudness, shown in how far the wave goes above or below the central line.

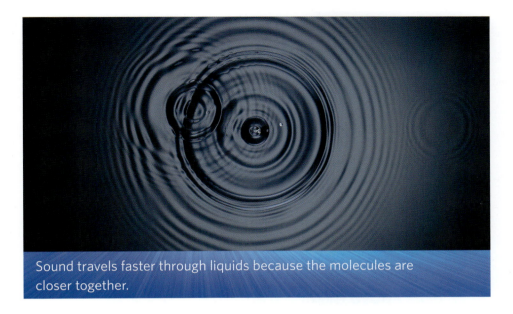

Sound travels faster through liquids because the molecules are closer together.

are closer together. Sound travels about four times faster through water than it does through air. That is why whales are able to communicate over very long distances.

Molecules in solids are extremely close together. When a sound wave hits one molecule, it can travel to the next molecule very quickly. Sound travels fastest of all through solids. For example, sound moves thirteen times faster through wood than it does through air.

FREQUENCY AND AMPLITUDE

Sound is measured in two different ways: **amplitude** and **frequency**. Amplitude measures how loud a sound is. Frequency measures a sound's **pitch**. Pitch is how high and squeaky or low and deep a sound is.

Think back to the waves you learned about in chapter 1. Imagine sound as a wave moving along a line. The wave rises above the line the same distance that it dips below. Both amplitude and frequency can be measured in these waves.

Amplitude is how far the wave goes up and down. The top of the wave is called the **crest**. The bottom of the wave is the trough. The higher the amplitude, the louder the sound.

Frequency is how fast the wave moves up and down. High frequency sounds move fast. These sounds are high-pitched, like a very small dog barking or most birds

SEEING SOUND

You can see sound with a simple experiment using common kitchen items. You will need:

Plastic wrap (enough to cover a bowl)
A medium to large bowl
A metal pan or cookie sheet
A metal spoon
One tablespoon of uncooked rice

Stretch the plastic wrap tightly over the bowl. Place rice on top of the plastic. Hold the metal pan close to the bowl. Hit the pan with the spoon. The sound vibrations from the banging will travel through the plastic wrap and make the rice bounce.

singing. Low frequency sounds are slow and deep, like a big dog barking or the instrument called a double bass.

When an object moves faster than the speed of sound, it makes a **sonic boom**. The speed of sound is about 761 miles per hour (1,225 kilometers per hour), but it can change depending on altitude and temperature. As a jet reaches the speed of sound, it catches up with

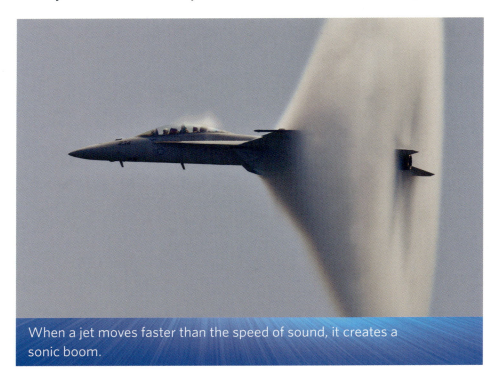

When a jet moves faster than the speed of sound, it creates a sonic boom.

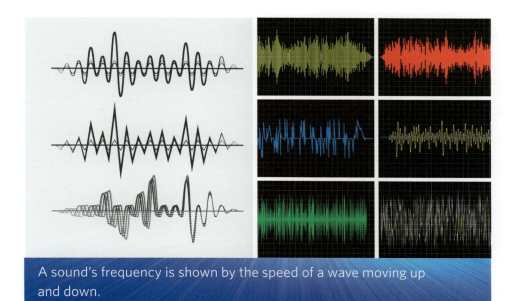

A sound's frequency is shown by the speed of a wave moving up and down.

the sound waves it is causing. This compresses them all into a single shock wave—the boom. Cracking a whip makes a tiny sonic boom. The tip moves so fast it breaks the sound barrier.

FAST FACT

Some sounds are too high or too low for us to hear. Sounds too high to hear are called **ultrasonic**. *Sounds too low to hear are called* **infrasonic**.

The Roman architect Vitruvius applied sound theories to theater design.

CHAPTER 3

SOUND DISCOVERIES

Some of the earliest scientists understood that sound moves in waves. In ancient Greece, a famous scientist and philosopher named Aristotle wrote about sound. Aristotle's theory was that "sound is a particular movement of air." In first-century Rome, an architect named Vitruvius said a sound moves like an ocean wave, flowing out from its source in all directions. These discoveries inspired many scientists to study sound.

MODERN SOUND TECHNOLOGY

In the twentieth century, scientists studied sound for new inventions. Sonar was first used in World War I to find enemy submarines. The earliest methods

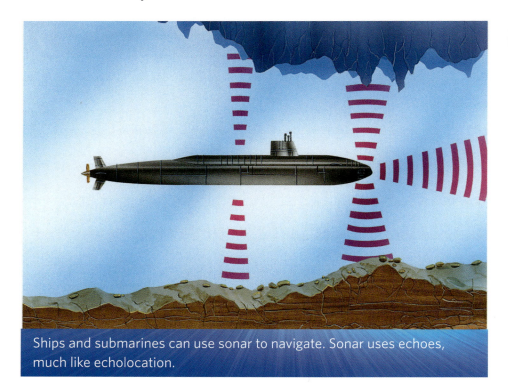

Ships and submarines can use sonar to navigate. Sonar uses echoes, much like echolocation.

Commercial fishing ships use sound to find huge schools of fish.

just listened for sounds that submarines made. As technology advanced, devices sent out sounds and listened for their echoes.

Modern sound technology impacts the world around us. Fishing boats use sound to find huge schools of fish. Sound helps fishermen to catch more fish.

Unfortunately, sound also creates the risk of overfishing. Whales and dolphins can also be harmed by sound. These animals use sonar, which can be damaged by military sound testing.

HOW SOUND WORKS IN TELEPHONES

One of the most popular uses for sound is in telephones. If you connect two metal cans with a string, pull the string tight, and speak into one end, the actual sound vibrations will travel along the string. You will hear the sound in the other can.

FAST FACT

The earliest recordings were made on tin- or wax-coated cylinders. Disks weren't used until 1881. The first disks were made of shellac, which is a natural material that looks like plastic. Later, record players used vinyl disks. Early disks used a needle to read grooves in the disk. Today, CDs and DVDs use lasers to read patterns on disks.

THOMAS EDISON

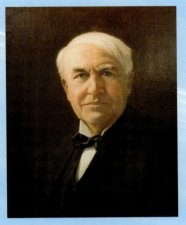
Portrait of Thomas Edison

The phonograph was invented by Thomas Edison in 1877. Edison was looking for a way to record telegraph messages. A telegraph is a device for sending signals along a wire. Only beeps are sent, not voices or other sounds. While thinking about this problem, he came up with the phonograph.

Sound was recorded by a needle tracing a pattern in tin. Sound vibrations made the needle move. Each sound made a unique pattern.

A phonograph

Edison used a second needle to trace the grooves made by the first. The vibrations made by the second needle helped turn the sound up louder. They copied the sound of a voice.

SOUND DISCOVERIES

However, in a real phone, sound has to travel over large distances. Sound vibrations can't travel along a telephone line. When someone speaks into a phone, the sound is changed to an electrical signal. An electrical signal can travel farther than sound waves. That signal travels to the other phone. There, the signals make a thin film vibrate. The electrical signal is turned back into sound waves, recreating the speaker's words.

In landline phones, sounds become electrical signals that travel over a wire.

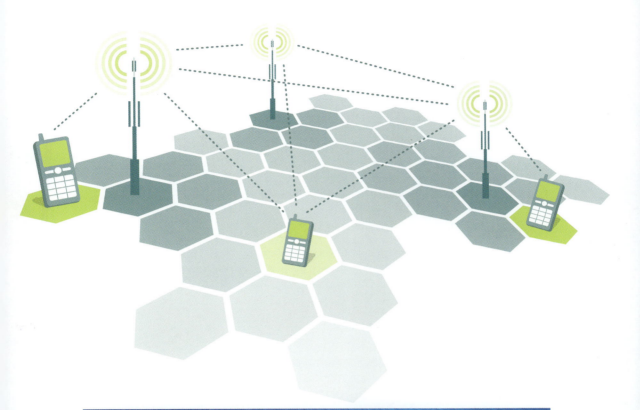

Cell phones work much like landline phones, but the sound is converted to radio waves.

A cell phone works in a similar way. Instead of using a wire, the signal is sent by radio waves through a network of cell towers.

HOW DOES IT MOVE QUIZ

Question 1: What does sound need to travel through?

Question 2: What is the measure of how far a sound wave goes up and down from the center line called?

Question 3: List at least one way in which sounds can harm animals or the environment.

Answer 1: Matter, or a medium, which can be gas, liquid, or solid.

Answer 2: Amplitude.

Answer 3: Using sonar to find fish schools can lead to overfishing; underwater sound experiments can damage whales' hearing and sonar, leading to strandings.

GLOSSARY

amplitude A measure of a sound's volume.

cochlea Part of the inner ear that receives sound vibrations.

ear canal A tunnel from the outside ear to the inner ear.

eardrum Part of the ear that vibrates from sound waves.

echo A sound caused by the bouncing back of sound waves.

frequency How quickly a sound wave moves up and down.

infrasonic A sound that is too low to hear.

matter Anything that takes up space.

medium Material sound moves through.

pitch A measure of how high or low a sound is.

sonar Technology that uses echoes to navigate.

sonic boom When an object moves faster than sound.

ultrasonic A sound that is too high to hear.

ultrasound Sound used in medicine to look inside the body.

vibration Up-and-down movement around a central line.

FIND OUT MORE

BOOKS

Basher, Simon, and Dan Green. *Basher Science: Physics: Why Matter Matters!* New York, NY: Kingfisher, 2016.

Frith, Margaret. *Who Was Thomas Alva Edison?* New York, NY: Penguin, 2005.

WEBSITES

Kids' Health: The Ears

http://kidshealth.org/en/kids/ears.html

See how physics and biology intersect in this interesting health site that explains how we hear. This site contains links to other ways sound and health work together, such as how loud sounds can damage ears.

Physics for Kids: Basics of Sound

http://www.ducksters.com/science/sound101.php

This section of Ducksters introduces kids to the science of sound and has links to many other pages within the site for further exploration.

INDEX

Page numbers in **boldface** *are illustrations.*

amplitude, **14**, 16
bats, 8, **9**
ear, 6–8, **6**, **7**
echoes, 8, 12
echolocation, 8
Edison, Thomas, 25, **25**
experiment, sound, 17
fishing, **23**, 23–24
frequency, 16–18, **19**
infrasonic, 19
matter, 13
medium, 13–15
music, 11–12
phonograph, 25, **25**
pitch, 16
recordings, 24–25
science, 12–13, 21–22
sonar, 12–13, 22, **22**
sonic boom, **18**, 18–19
sound waves, 6, **6**, **14**, 14–16, 19, 21
speed of sound, 18
submarines, **22**, 22–23
telephones, 24–27, **26**, **27**
ultrasonic, 19
ultrasound, 13, **13**
vibrations, 5–7, 9, 11–13, 17, 24–26
vocal cords, 12, **12**
whales, 8, **8**, 15

ABOUT THE AUTHOR

Laura L. Sullivan is the author of more than forty fiction and nonfiction books for children, including the fantasies *Under the Green Hill* and *Guardian of the Green Hill*. She lives in Florida, where she likes to bike, hike, kayak, hunt fossils, and practice Brazilian jiu jitsu.